# THE RESURRECTION

This publication marks the first annual
***Mary Milligan RSHM Lecture in Spirituality.***
The series is made possible by the generous donations of
friends of the Religious of the Sacred Heart of Mary and
Loyola Marymount University,
with many thanks to all who made this possible.

Mary Genino, RSHM
Provincial Superior of the Western American Province of
the Religious of the Sacred Heart of Mary

# The Resurrection
## Did it Really Happen and Why Does That Matter?

Sandra M. Schneiders, IHM

The Resurrection: Did it really happen and why does that matter?
Copyright © 2013 by Sandra M. Schneiders, IHM. All rights reserved.

ISBN: 978-0-9839616-8-0

First Edition: April, 2013

Marymount Institute Press,
a Tsehai Publishers Imprint, Loyola Marymount University,
One LMU Drive, Suite 3012, Los Angeles, CA 90045

www.tsehaipublishers.com/mip
mip@tsehaipublishers.com

Publisher: Elias Wondimu
Editor: Theresia de Vroom, Ph.D.
Guest Associate Editor: Michael Horan, Ph.D.
Cover Design: Eugene Groisman
Layout Design: Sara Martinez and Ann Park

Apart from any fair dealing for the purpose of private study, research, criticism or review, as permitted under the Copyright Act, no part of this publication may be reproduced in any form, stored in a retrieval system or transmitted in any form by any means—electronic, mechanical, photocopy, recording or otherwise—without the prior permission of the publisher. Enquiries should be sent to the undermentioned address.

Marymount Institute Press and Tsehai Publishers books
may be purchased for educational, business, or sales promotional use.
For more information, please contact our special sales department.

## Contents

| | |
|---|---:|
| Acknowledgements | vi |
| Foreword, David W. Burcham | 1 |
| The Resurrection | |
|    I   Introduction | 7 |
|    II   What Happened and Why is it Significant? | 9 |
|    III   How Do We Know? | 15 |
|    IV   The Resurrection in Text and in Fact | 33 |
|    V   Conclusion | 45 |
|    VI   Notes | 47 |
| Contributors | 52 |

## ACKNOWLEDGEMENTS

The Marymount Institute Press would like to thank all the contributors to this book. We would also like to thank the many individuals who made it possible for this book to come to fruition. Firstly, Sister Mary Genino RSHM, Provincial Superior, and the Religious of the Sacred Heart of Mary of the Western American Province for their generous support.

The artist, Will Pupa, Artist in Residence for the Marymount Institute and Clinical Professor of Art, for his extraordinary contribution to the artistic life of the University as well as this book. Eugene Grossman, for always designing the perfect cover. Michael Horan, Professor of Theological Studies and Guest Associate Editor for this volume, who knows a thing or two about the "harrowing of hell"; Jonathan Rothchild, Associate Professor and Chair of Theological Studies, and Fr. James Fredericks, Professor of Theology.

Our student interns, Sara Martinez and Ann Park, and our Graduate Assistants, Will Gish and Darcey Whitmore. Chake Kouyoumjian, Associate Dean of Graduate Studies for her continued support. Logan Metz for his editorial assistance. And Sandra M. Schnieders, for writing this magnificent essay and meeting an hair-raising deadline with generosity and grace.

We thank the Advisory Board for the Marymount Institute, in particular the Chair of the Board, Dr. Lane Bove, Senior Vice President for Student Affairs. The support of Joseph Hellige, Provost has been crucial to everything we do, as is the support of the President of the University, David W. Burcham.

|  |  |
|---|---|
| Theresia de Vroom | Elias Wondimu |
| Editor | Publisher |

One of the striking characteristics of Father Gailhac's spirituality is his insistence on authenticity, on congruence between what we say and what we live. Our faith is a faith which should *manifest itself*; our love for others must be effective.

> Mary Milligan, RSHM
> *From a letter to her community*
> February 24, 1982

# FOREWORD

It is an honor and a pleasure to write this brief foreword to publication of the first Mary Milligan Lecture in Spirituality by Mary's distinguished colleague, collaborator, and dear friend, Sandra M. Schneiders, IHM.

I want to contextualize Mary's life and contribution in the rich theological and spiritual tradition she lived. Mary Milligan was shaped by the theological currents of Vatican II, and in turn, she greatly influenced the renewal of religious life in the trajectory of the Council. Specifically Sr. Mary influenced the Religious of the Sacred Heart of Mary through her leadership, and she extended the spirituality of RSHM to a wide readership through her writings. Her teaching, speaking, scholarship and leadership placed the principles of Vatican II squarely at the center of thought and action.

Two driving principles of Vatican Council II were enunciated in two words, one French, the other Italian. The principle of *ressourcement* –return to the sources –drove the bishops and their theological advisors to return and research the earliest Christian period and to mine the sources of scripture and earliest Christian era for their insight into how to live a Christian life. The second word, *aggiornamento*, or "bringing up to date," became the Italian watchword for Pope John XXIII as expressed through his inspiring speech at the opening session of Vatican II. In the face of unprecedented human misery and a globe threatened by the potential of nuclear war, Pope John insisted that "today it is only dawn" and that the best of human history lies ahead.

The task of the Council, in Pope John's view, was not like the task of other Councils – he did not call the Council in order to address a problem or to condemn its perpetrators. Rather, John XXIII's iconic gesture of "opening of the window" instructed the church and its leaders to look into the world to find God, to be renewed and updated by encountering and learning from the world, not by fleeing from it or condemning it. The driving principles of ressourcement and aggiornamento opened the intellectual and spiritual spaces for the Council's leaders and their advisors to fill their imaginations, and eventually the Council documents, with words that communicated the ideals of these two principles.

Through her religious life, her studies in Europe, her research and teaching career, Mary Milligan RSHM employed these principles. Her work in the history of religious life illustrates the principles as they were elaborated in *Perfectae Caritatis* ("On the Renewal of Religious Life"). Her writing on spirituality and the bible reflects the emphases found in *Dei Verbum* ("Dogmatic Constitution on Divine Revelation"). Her theological research and teaching, like her community leadership, faithfully and creatively echoed the critical purchase of these two principles at work in the late 20th century.

Knowing one's deeply rooted identity requires careful historical analysis and the courage to interpret the present moment. Mary understood early and clearly that the Catholic Church and its apostolic religious communities could be renewed to the degree that they at once echoed and answered the clarion call of the Gospel to place all of us at the service of the poor and marginalized. Mary's writing, speaking, leading, befriending, and her sisterhood drew people closer to this insight and the commitment it demands. She taught generations of students and colleagues, by word and example, that authentic disciples of Christ share in their "joy and hope, the grief and anguish" of all people, but especially the poor, and there find God.

Here at Loyola Marymount University, the intersection of faith, culture and the arts embodied by the Marymount Institute offers one meeting place for authentic conversations about the meaning of life and the presence of the holy in the earthly. Theological Studies reflects on that presence and action of God in the world, and critically analyzes it. Mary Milligan knew this through Theology, art, culture and cultures, and thanks to her work among us, we know it better. Her words remind us of the richness of her mind and the depth of her commitment. We let them speak for her.

*Taken from letters to the Religious of the Sacred Heart of Mary written by Mary Milligan when she was General Superior, 1980-1985.*

The disciples of Jesus—today as in the past—are called to break bread and to hear the word with others in the community. No one is a disciple in isolation.

The story of [our foundress] Appollonie Cure..is both illuminating and inspiring….She did not see the death of her husband as an event altering the divine plan for her. She focused not on the discontinuity of her life but on the continuity of God's call through the tragic circumstances of "bellowed Eugene's" death. She saw her vocation to religious life as a great grace—grace obtained by the prayer of her husband. "I firmly believe that it is his beautiful soul which obtained this great grace for me" (September, 18, 1849). She referred to the loss of her husband as the "great sorrow which I could not have borne had not God called me to such a beautiful vocation" (October 15, 1849).

Our foundress's ability to read God's word in her life, her generosity in responding to that work are certainly a precious heritage for us…..The demands of such a vocation are many….It seems to me, however, that an attitude of "listening as a disciple" is basic to our response to these demands. To discover the Lord's call in the concrete situations of our life, we must be able to *hear* that call and to *verify* it in order to *act* on it.

*February 24, 1982*

Obedience to law can never be a substitute for freedom and responsibility. Our very obedience must be a free and responsible act. Conscience must always be ultimately decisive—conscience which [is] "the sanctuary of creative fidelity and liberty".

*February 24, 1983*


John Paul II's encyclical, *Dives in Misericordia*, using a free translation of Psalm 85, speaks of the *kiss* which gives mercy to justice. It says…that there is no true justice without mercy. Because of our…commitment to "be at the service of evangelical justice wherever we are", this letter on mercy is of great importance to us…..[John Paul II] sees mercy as "the most perfect incarnation of 'equality' between people" and therefore, the most perfect incarnation of justice.

It seems to me that the "kiss of justice and mercy" is symbolic of the love that is the source of both of those realities. In some sense, both justice and mercy are love, just as both faith and zeal are. When love stands before a situation of injustice, it acts and that action is just. Justice is love thirsting for the recognition of human dignity of all people. Where any one's basic human rights are infringed upon, where one's God-given dignity is not recognized, there "evangelical justice"—a justice which springs from love….

*February 24, 1981*


We have seen and continue to see injustices within the Church. The earthen vessels in which the treasure of holiness is carried are always in need of purification. We have at times seemed to walk on uncertain waters, and may have genuinely cried: "Save us Lord, we are perishing."

*May, 1981*


…there are three women of faith that we might invoke as our intercessors in a special way….

The first is…Sarah. Both sterile and aged, she learned that she would bear a child. [She is] remembered by future generations as an extraordinary example of faith: By faith,. Sarah herself received the power to conceive, even when she was past the age, since she considered him faithful who had promised" (Hebrews, 11:11).

The transition from the Old to the New Testament is made by Elizabeth, another woman "advanced in age" and sterile. Humiliated by her sterility, as was Sarah, she praises God when she does conceive. Again, like Sarah, she believes that the Lord's promises to her will be fulfilled.

And it is precisely for this faith in God's promise that she praises her cousin Mary (Luke, 1:45). Mary too has believed that, though she "had no husband", she would bear a child, her YES in faith *was* her mission, was itself the instrument through which the Christian future was created.

Scripture constantly shows God acting through sterile women. It is surely not sterility itself which saves, but faith that nothing is too hard, too marvelous for the Lord (Genesis 18:14; Luke 1:34)…. Let us call on these three women of faith—Sarah, Elizabeth and especially Mary. Let us learn from them that…the lack of human means is the situation *par excellence* where God can work marvels for the good of the world and the Church.

*May 24, 1984*

We join together in the spirit of Mary Millligan RSHM, in the meaning of the Resurrection, knowing "That all may have life."

David W. Burcham
President
Loyola Marymount University
4 April 2013

# Introduction

It is not only an honor but a consolation and a joy to be able to remember and honor my dear friend, Mary Milligan, RSHM, by this inaugural lecture just two years after Mary's death. And it gives me special joy that this celebration of Mary's life occurs during Easter week, on the very day we read in the liturgy the remarkable story of two grief-stricken disciples who have just lost t their dearest friend, Jesus. As they make their despairing way home from Jerusalem, site of Jesus' execution, they are joined unawares by the Risen Jesus himself who initiates them and, through them, us into the experience that Mary now enjoys in all its fullness and that we will be exploring this evening, the Risen Jesus' real bodily presence to, among, and in his post-Easter disciples.

I entitled this lecture not, as one usually does, with a declarative sentence stating the thesis I will develop, but with a twofold question which my experience in ministry tells me is very much alive in many people who are believing and practicing Christians, who sincerely profess every week in the creed their faith in the bodily Resurrection of Jesus, but who draw an imaginative blank when they try to put modern, scientifically credible flesh on these theological bones. In what follows I hope to offer some resources for reflecting on the problem for Christian faith of the imaginative implausibility of bodily resurrection.[1] The first question, "Did the Resurrection of Jesus really happen?" is about the FACT of the mystery. If nothing happened on Easter, that is the end of story. However, if what we confess is something that did happen, our very lives pivot around that happening and unfolding its SIGNIFICANCE, that is, what it means for the believer, is crucial.

It probably will not destroy the suspense for you to know in advance that I am going to answer, "yes" to the question of fact. Something happened. But in order to unfold the significance of that we have to inquire specifically into WHAT happened? And then we can ask, HOW what happened is available to or communicated to and received by us? That is, how do we know that something happened, what happened, and why it matters? But all this is only necessary scaffolding for what we are really interested in, namely, how the Resurrection transforms our life, or as Paul would say, makes our faith truly alive and life giving.

# WHAT HAPPENED AND WHY IS IT SIGNIFICANT?

Let me rephrase the question, "What happened on Easter?" a little more clearly. We are really asking, what does it mean to say that Christ is risen? Does it mean that he is immortal, a spirit alive with God somewhere outside earthly time and space (which most Christians believe is true of all who die in faith), or did something unique, that has happened to no one else, happen to Jesus on the first Easter?[2] And, if so, what was it and why is this unique event significant for us?

I am going to invite you to think through these questions with me, in a somewhat new way from what we are used to when we read treatments of the Resurrection in some catechetical presentations or even theological studies. My basic hypothesis is that the problem most people encounter in regard to the Resurrection is not in their faith but in the ways we moderns, especially since the Enlightenment,[3] have learned to think about reality, and above all to imagine the real. We have been taught that it is our discursive mind that gives us access to the truth and truth is the correspondence of our mind to a freestanding factual, that is, objective, reality, like a traffic accident, that is outside of us and independent of our opinions about it.

But when it comes to certain kinds of truth, it is actually our imagination which constructs the world in which we live and move and have our being and within which we participate in reality less factually and more holistically than we tend to think we do. We do not know what it means to be family or to be in love the way we know that a traffic accident occurred on the corner of Elm and Main or that certain chemicals, if combined, will explode. But being family, being in love is every bit as real. In other words, not all truth is scientifically or experimentally verifiable. Some very real reality is only available to the holistic operations of the imagination.

Many treatments of the Resurrection, however, approach it objectively with factual questions about what really happened on Easter morning and in the following weeks. I want to suggest an imaginative approach to the Resurrection, which is emphatically not an experiment in fantasy because imagination is not fantasy. But imagination is also not about establishing objective facts like the details of a traffic accident. It is a way of entering a new world, one that really exists and that we have excellent reasons to believe in and live in, but not the kind of reasons we have learned to trust in thinking about what we tend to call "objective" reality or something that "really happened."

So, to our first set of questions: What happened on Easter and why is it significant or, more simply: What do we really believe about the Resurrection? Why does Paul say that if the Resurrection did not happen Christianity is empty, pointless, vain, and we are still in our sins (cf. 1 Cor. 15:17)?

First, as we all know, being a Christian is not primarily about morality, or our relation to Church authority, or dogmas, or even the role of the Christian in the transformation of the world. All these things are important, but when a Scribe asked Jesus what was really basic, primary, non-negotiable, the most important commandment, Jesus replied "The first is, ...you shall love the Lord your God with [your whole being].... and, [equally important] you must love your neighbor as yourself." The Scribe replied, "You are right, Teacher...this is much more important than all whole burnt offerings and sacrifices", in other words, more than all religious teachings and practices. And Jesus returned the compliment by saying to the Scribe, "You are not far from the Kingdom of God" (see Mk. 12:28-34).[4] In other words, "You are right!"

But the connection between love of God and love of neighbor for the Christian is Jesus. In John's Gospel Jesus says, "No one has ever seen God. It is God the only Son.... who has made God known" (see Jn. 1:18). In other words, it is Jesus, the Son of God incarnate, who reveals the true God to us by pointing to himself: "I and the Father are one" (see Jn. 10:30) he says, and "whoever sees me sees the One who sent me" (see Jn. 12:45; 14:9). And, when the Risen Jesus personally encountered Paul on the road to Damascus, he answered Paul's question, "Who are you, Lord?" with "I am Jesus whom you are persecuting" (Acts 9:5).

In this brief synopsis of the heart of Christian faith, love of God who is manifested in Jesus and love of neighbor who is Jesus' presence to us, you note that the verbs are in the present tense: Whoever sees me, sees God and I am Jesus whom you are persecuting. So we are not talking about some theological theory of the Trinity or about some kind of pious make-believe by which we pretend that our neighbor is Jesus. The Christian is one who, here and now, sees Jesus and relates to God in him; who here and now, in relating to the neighbor, relates to Jesus himself.

Furthermore, the one in whom all Christian faith and life are centered is not simply the Christ, but Jesus. Christ, or Messiah, is not Jesus' last name; it is Jesus' "job description," a title denoting his role in salvation history. When we say "Jesus" we are talking about a first century Jew who lived in Palestine, who was the Son of Mary and Joseph of Nazareth. In other words, Christian faith is centered in Jesus who is here and now alive and who is a very specific human being who is not reducible to his role or functions in salvation history, who was not transformed at death into some kind of abstract omega point of history or some kind of cosmic energy, who is not simply a disembodied immortal spirit. However, because we know that Jesus of Nazareth died by crucifixion under Pontius Pilate in Palestine sometime around 30 CE and was buried in a tomb that was securely sealed, we can only talk about him as personally present to us and in us and among us here and now if he personally overcame death and is now alive. In short, the first thing we mean by our faith confession in the Resurrection is that Jesus is personally alive.

The second thing, which is really the negative way of stating the first, concerns what we are not saying. The focus of our faith is not the ongoing influence or example of someone who once lived like Paul or Teresa of Avila but died and is no longer among us. Nor is our faith commitment to a great project initiated by Jesus in the past, which continues today like the Civil Rights Movement initiated by Martin Luther King, Jr. and Rosa Parks. Nor is our faith membership in a community which gathers around the memory of Jesus the way fans of Elvis Presley gather at Graceland. Although an ongoing historical influence, a great world-transforming project, and a community, that is Christianity, are indeed rooted in Jesus, what we confess by the Resurrection is that Jesus himself, in his specific and personal identity, is alive and present here and now. Without him, the memory, the project, and the community may be very real but they are rootless. And that means we are necessarily talking about Jesus' bodily resurrection because a human being, a person in the full integrity of their humanity, does not just have a body, but is their body. Therefore, integral Christian spirituality depends on Jesus being not just personally alive but bodily risen from the dead and accessible to us.

The reason why the fact that Jesus is bodily risen from the dead is significant is at least threefold. First, it means that a real, mortal human being passed through human death and emerged into new life as himself, returned to his own, and now lives in the fullness of his humanity in God. No other religion makes such a claim. So we have no historical or theological analogues for understanding it. That is the reason Paul met with such incredulity among his Corinthian (see 1 Cor. 15) and later his Athenian (see Acts 17:1-34) hearers. What Paul was preaching, and what we preach today, is unparalleled among world religions. The Resurrection of Jesus inserted something absolutely new, unprecedented, and unique into human history, which affects each of us personally.

We will all pass through the portal of human mortality. Real death is the only way out of this life. But, as Jesus said to Martha about her dead and buried brother Lazarus, whose mortal body had already begun to decay, in other words, who was irrevocably dead: "Those who believe in me, even though they die, will live, and everyone who lives and believes in me will never die" precisely because Jesus "is the resurrection and the life" (see Jn. 11:25-26). In the Risen Jesus humanity itself has entered fully and definitively into the infinite and indestructible life of the Trinity and thus we, after our own real and personal death, will share bodily in that victory, not as ghosts or shadows or disembodied immortal souls or some kind of participant in cosmic energy, but as our own embodied human selves. In other words, the first reason why Jesus' bodily resurrection is significant is that the Resurrection of Jesus is the assurance and basis of our own bodily resurrection, which is not something we can deduce from any experience or reasoning process available to us.

Second, the living Jesus is not only present and living in God, but is among his followers, his community, now making them his real corporate presence in the world. "Wherever two or three are gathered in my name, there am I in their midst" (Mt. 18:20), Jesus assured them. Jesus' bodiliness is not only his personal embodiment, but he is the unifying and identifying principle of his corporate bodiliness. As Paul said, "Now you are the body of Christ and individually members of it" (1 Cor. 12:27). The community of believers is the presence of Jesus acting in the world, doing, as John's Gospel says, "even greater things" than the pre-Easter Jesus himself did (see Jn. 14:12). So the second aspect of the significance of the bodily Resurrection is that Jesus is alive and present in the world and we, his body, participate in his ongoing salvific work, not just by imitating him the way we might imitate St. Francis of Assisi or Mother Teresa but because we are his real bodily presence.

Third, the living, bodily risen Jesus is not only present in God, present in the world through his members who are his body, but also present in his individual followers. Jesus said to his disciples, even as he was about to depart from them in death, "My going away is my coming to you" (Jn. 14:28).[5] "Abide in me as I abide in you" (Jn. 15:4). This mutual indwelling of Jesus in the believer and the believer in Jesus, which is a present reality, is the source of the disciple's life and fruitfulness; the basis of a personal, experiential union with Jesus which is meant to develop over a lifetime until it is consummated in the fullness of resurrection life after death.

In summary, Resurrection faith is the conviction THAT Jesus is bodily risen from death and now lives in the full integrity of his humanity in God, in the world through his body which his disciples corporately are, and in each believer who, therefore, is and acts in persona Christi, while growing in personal union with Jesus which will be fully realized in the disciple's own eventual bodily resurrection from the dead. This is what Paul wanted his converts to realize, that the Resurrection of Jesus was the key to everything Christianity had to offer them. If Jesus is not risen, Christianity is one religion among others, a possible basis for a good, even heroic, human life, but not at all what Paul was preaching to them and to us. Christianity is not one religion among others because it believes something about Jesus that has no parallel in any other religion.

This Resurrection spirituality is testified to by virtually all the great saints of the Christian tradition beginning with Mary Magdalene and Paul, through Francis of Assisi and Teresa of Avila, down to Thomas Merton and Dorothy Day. And interestingly enough, it is not only simple believers but also the greatest mystics and theologians, people who had the tools to debunk religious credulity or pious make-believe, who speak most clearly about the vividness of their personal experience of the living Jesus and his centrality to their spirituality.

# HOW DO WE KNOW?

If this is what Christians believe about the Resurrection and it is of ultimate significance for their identity as Christians, indeed what makes Christians Christian, we have to ask the question that challenges many modern people, namely, "If there are no analogues for this faith, how do we know that what we believe is true?" Of course, one perfectly good answer is that we know it because the Church teaches it and since we believe the Church is the, or at least a, reliable mediator between us and God, we accept this teaching, along with many others, as true.

But actually, the real question lurking in the "How do we know?" is not about whether it makes sense to accept what we are taught by someone we consider trustworthy. We do this all the time. The real question is how this faith can come to life in our experience, how we can actually understand it. I can know that I am a member of a family because if I were not, in some sense, a member of a family I would not be here. I have a mother and a father. Someone from the records department might even be able to tell me, quite authoritatively, who they are. But if I have never met them, never experienced their attitudes toward me, do not share life and experience with them, "my family" remains a very abstract concept. I believe it. And it is quite reasonable to believe it. But it does not do much for me existentially. Indeed, it may even be more destructive than life giving precisely because, knowing theoretically what a family really is, I know what I am missing. The real way to know family is to live it, to experience it. That experience is what constitutes the imaginative world of family as opposed to the theoretical, or "objective" one. The question is, how does the world of the Resurrection become real and operative, rather than simply a credal proposition, for the contemporary Christian?

# *The Problem of the Historical Approach to the Resurrection*

Even if it is clear that the early Church and the whole of our tradition testifies to the fact of the bodily Resurrection of Jesus and its ultimate significance in the life of the believer, the contemporary Christian, by which I mean those of us who live in the intellectual world created by the Scientific Revolution and the Enlightenment and who live our faith among people who do not share that faith, is very much tempted to push this question into the scientifically historical realm in search of objective warrants for what we believe. For at least a couple centuries scholars and ordinary believers alike, who are willing to affirm the Resurrection as something they "take on faith," continue to be plagued by this issue of "proof," that is, of public warrants for their faith, a way of understanding it which can make sense to people for whom it is not a matter of faith because one of the best guarantees that what we hold is actually true is our ability to prove it, or at least make it plausible, to someone else who has no vested interests in accepting it.

The science-inspired modern questions bear on the experience of the Easter witnesses, which, in one way or another, are presented as warrants for faith in the Resurrection and sources of knowledge about what actually happened to Jesus after his death. Was the tomb really empty and if so does that prove anything about what happened to Jesus? What really happened to the first witnesses on Easter morning and in the following days? Did they really see or hear or touch something or someone? With their bodily senses or only by faith or in their desperate fantasies? And if they did actually experience something, what was it? Might they have been hallucinating, or deceived by wishful thinking, even making it all up for worthy or unworthy motives?

These questions cannot be finessed, ruled out of court as the challenge of heretics, agnostics, or infidels. They are the reasonable questions of people who want their faith to be, not necessarily apodictically proven, but to be "imaginatively implausible." We live in a scientific world which distinguishes between, on the one hand, facts which can be objectively established by repeatable experiments, or multiple attestation of witnesses, or historical investigation of reliable sources and, on the other hand, personal opinions, naïve pious beliefs, hallucinations, or wishful thinking on the other. We live in an world in which Christianity is not the only credible religion and in which other religions, and even agnosticism or atheism, produce people just as admirable, often more so, than Christians, and who get along quite well without any idea of the personal bodily resurrection of Jesus, to say nothing of his living presence in the world today. We live in a world in which our own experience suggests that dead people stay dead and that even the unusual experiences some people may have of their beloved (or feared) dead can usually be explained psychologically or, at least, are so idiosyncratic and that they have no significance for our general worldview including the issue of life after death. And if truth be told, except for the celebration of Easter, many of the Christians most of us associate with would be hard put to say what, if any, effect the Resurrection has on their day-to-day life. Would it make any real difference to the way they (or we) live if Jesus, like our deceased relatives and friends, were somehow with God as we all hope to be some day, but not, in some absolutely unique way, bodily risen from the dead and still alive among and in us?

I am going to try to identify and subvert some epistemological assumptions that function, quite understandably, in most discussions of the Resurrection but that set us up for thinking in ways that necessarily rule out the kind of understanding of Resurrection that I have just claimed is central to our faith. Because the Church preaches that "Jesus rose from the dead," in the same kind of sentence we use to say that "There was a car accident on the corner of Elm and Main," it is easy to assume that a similar claim is being made in both cases, namely, that we are talking about an historical, publicly available event, caused by observable or ascertainable factors like someone running a red light or the brakes failing. There are several reasons to call into question this assumption about what "event" means or what it means to say that something really "happened."

Our sources of knowledge about the Resurrection are of two kinds. The oldest are proclamations of the fact and meaning of the Resurrection, like Paul's account in 1 Cor. 15: 3ff: "For I handed on to you as of first importance what I in turn had received: that Christ died for our sins in accordance with the scriptures, and that he was buried, and that he was raised on the third day in accordance with the scriptures, and that he appeared to Cephas, then to the twelve...." followed by his conclusion: "If Christ has not been raised, your faith is futile and you are still in your sins." Similar proclamations are made in the apostolic sermons in the Acts of the Apostles, for example, Peter's proclamation, "this man, handed over to you according to the definite plan and foreknowledge of God, you crucified and killed by the hands of those outside the law. But God raised him up, having freed him from death, because it was impossible for him to be held in its power" (Acts 2:23-24 ff).

Much later we have the narratives of the Easter events, from the end of each Gospel such as the stories of the empty tomb and Jesus' appearances to Mary Magdalene, to the disciples on the way to Emmaus, to "Doubting Thomas," to the disciples in the upper room, and so on. Most people think the proclamations were short forms, summaries, of the narratives and that our faith is really based on the narratives that are presented as the factual accounts of the Resurrection event. But actually, it is the other way around. The gospel narratives are the long forms of the proclamations. The narratives were written later than the proclamations and are not historical narratives like the accounts of the Crucifixion. In other words, whatever they are, the appearance narratives are not like traffic reports. They are a different kind of literature and we need to attend to how they can, should, and do function in our faith in the Resurrection.

Because the Resurrection Narratives are stories and they follow the stories which recount the public life of Jesus, we naturally read them as the "final chapter" in Jesus' historical life. After his mysterious conception, miraculous birth, and his virtually un-narrated childhood and youth in Nazareth (Chapter 1), Jesus undertook a short public life of preaching, working miracles, and forming his disciples by which he became a threat to the Roman political authorities who ruled Palestine, and to the Jewish religious hierarchy (Chapter 2). These two power systems colluded to arrest him, condemn him to death, and execute him by crucifixion (Chapter 3). His disciples buried him before the beginning of Sabbath (Chapter 4). Then he rose from the dead and appeared to his disciples (Chapter 5).

Actually, the Resurrection is not Chapter Five at all. The Resurrection Narratives are a completely different kind of literature, or different genre, from the accounts of Chapters two, three, and four. The public life, passion and death, and burial are intended to recount the historical life of Jesus of Nazareth as it could have been and was observed by anyone, believer or not, who was present for the events that took place. The Gospels are, of course, suffused with profound theological reflection on, and the interpretation of, the significance of these events— but the events themselves are basically historical. They took place in time and space and according to the laws of cause and effect which operate in all historical events. We even have some references to some of these events from secular literature outside the Christian scriptures.

But the Resurrection Narratives are more like the Infancy Narratives, which are not Chapter One any more than the Resurrection is Chapter Five. Both the beginning and end of Jesus' life make mysterious connections between Jesus and God that are recounted as if they were historical in the normal sense of the word when in fact they are not. The Infancy Narratives are not our concern here but I mention them for purposes of comparison. They are written in a genre somewhat like that which scholars call midrash.[6] And Mark's Gospel, in fact, has no account at all of Jesus prior to his adult appearance at the Jordan for the beginning of his public life. Likewise, John's Gospel has no Infancy narrative but a theological Prologue identifying Jesus as the Word of God made flesh. We might say that the Infancy Narratives of Matthew and Luke, which are history-like stories, are to the mystery of the Incarnation or the becoming human of the Son of God, what the history-like Easter Narratives are to the mystery of the Resurrection or the overcoming of death in Jesus.

Both the Incarnation and the Resurrection in themselves are, what some scholars have called, "transhistorical events." Underlying the Infancy Narratives is the historical fact that Jesus was born. Without that fact there would be no story to tell. But, while the tapestry of angelic announcements and prophetic dreams, a star guiding the Magi from the east bearing symbolic gifts, a wicked king slaying all the infant boys in the Jerusalem area, or the census of Caesar Augustus, and so on, may have some historical "fringes," details or elements which can be verified historically, the point of the narratives is not to recount history, but to tell the reader, primarily by Old Testament allusions, who Jesus of Nazareth really is. The Incarnation itself, as opposed to the historical event of Jesus' birth, that is the becoming human as the Son of God, is a transhistorical reality, available only to faith.

And like the Incarnation, the Resurrection is a transhistorical event. At its heart is the reality that Jesus, who really died on the cross, is in and among his disciples in an entirely new way. Without this fact there would be no story to tell once Jesus was dead and buried. But the Easter Narratives in which this faith reality, the Resurrection is carried, are not stories like those of Jesus' public life and passion. Like the Infancy Narratives, the Easter Narratives are about something that is the object, not of physical observation, but of faith, which is woven into history in such a way that there are history-like details and historical fringes (like the conversations between the women and the male disciples on their return from the tomb), which give us access to what we believe, namely, that the crucified Jesus is alive and interacting with his disciples.

Why is this question of genre, or literary form, so important? Because we read texts in terms of what kind, that is, what genre, of text, we think they are. If we are reading a news article we will not excuse errors of fact. If we are reading a short story we expect verisimilitude but not necessarily historical facts. If we think a text is meant to be history, we expect it to be factual in the sense of objectively verifiable or at least based on facts that are, in principle, verifiable. So, if we think the Resurrection Narratives are Chapter Five of a biography or history of the earthly Jesus, we expect the Resurrection Narratives to be historical in the sense of telling us basically what really happened in time and space that would be observable by anyone present at the site of the occurrence, the same way a traffic accident could be seen by anyone who was on the corner of Elm and Main when it happened.

Starting basically in the Renaissance,[7] the study of historical texts began to be what we now call "historical critical" investigation. This way of studying texts was gradually extended from the pagan classics to the biblical texts. The use of historical critical methods entailed subscribing to certain presuppositions about the nature of historical texts and their relation to their subject matter which was presumed to be "what really happened." Such study, eventually called "the higher criticism," involved learning the original languages in which the historical text was composed, studying comparative history, understandings and practices of authorship, ancient geography, archaeology, literary genres, and so on. By the nineteenth century there was a fairly general consensus, at least among Protestant biblical scholars, who were followed in the mid-twentieth century by Catholic scholars, that such historical critical methodology was the most appropriate, and many people thought, the only modern and credible way to study the Bible.

This kind of historical critical study was first applied to the Old Testament, a treasure-trove of all kinds of literature posing all kinds of fascinating questions such as: "who wrote what, when, for what purpose?" and, does this literature tell us anything about "what really happened"? Did history-like stories, like the seven-day creation of the universe, the Flood, the Exodus, and Jonah's adventure in the belly of the whale, really happen as recounted? And that led to questions of whether, in some cases, such things happened at all. And finally to questions about the questions: is it important whether something happened as recounted, or happened at all, or is the pertinent question, why this story was included in the Bible and, if its point is not history, what might its point be? We know the kinds of conflicts in Christianity, some of which are very alive to this day such as creationism vs. evolution, which were generated by what we now call the modern historical critical study of the Old Testament. It took more than a century for scholars to dare to apply these same historical methods to the New Testament because the theological stakes for Christians were much higher. Jonah's adventure in the whale seemed much less critical for the Christian faith than the virginal conception of Jesus or whether Jesus actually did miracles like opening the eyes of the blind or walking on water.

What is important for our purposes here is not the historical methods scholars developed, but the fact that historical criticism was based on the seemingly obvious presupposition that everything written about the past, unless it was clearly poetry or fiction, was historical in the sense that our traffic accident is. That is, it happened. Anyone present could have seen it. It had ascertainable and publicly verifiable causes. The way to find out what is important about such an historical event begins with finding out what really happened. The way to do that, in relation to the past as today, is by looking at the physical and other types of evidence: questioning eye-witnesses if they are available or reading their accounts, comparing seemingly conflicting accounts, studying records, and, in modern times, looking at photos, coroners' reports, mechanics' diagnostics, and so on.

In the historical critical framework therefore, the important questions about biblical texts concerning the past are focused first of all on what really happened. Are we really descended from an original single couple? Was there really an Exodus from Egypt? Was Mary a virgin when Jesus was conceived? Did Jesus really walk on water? And to our point, was the tomb really empty on Easter morning? Did anyone actually see Jesus alive after his death? In other words, historical critical study was not only a method for studying historical material; it had become the criterion of what could be studied scientifically, namely, real historical facts, and what was worth studying, namely, things that really happened. Other objects were designated myths or fictions or projections or unprovable religious faith claims, all outside the scope of scientific study even if supremely important to faith. Today biblical scholars are very interested in other kinds of literature in Scripture, even though they continue to ask historical questions about almost everything. So, they might be very aware that a parable is not an historical account of something that really happened, such as a man being mugged on the road from Jerusalem to Jericho, but it is still important to ask whether Jesus actually told that parable and what it meant in the first century middle-eastern historical context in which it was told.

One can see where this leads in the case of material like the Infancy Narratives and the Resurrection Narratives. It became very important in regard to the former, for example, to establish whether there was an astronomical phenomenon sometime between 4 BCE and 6 CE which might have been the Magi's star and if so, whether that helps us determine the exact date of Jesus' birth, and so on. And it was very important to know whether Jesus appeared to the two disciples on the way to Emmaus and even whether one of the two might have been a woman.

Not surprisingly, historical critical study of the New Testament has led to an enormous amount of scholarly work on Resurrection Narratives,[8] precisely because faith in the Resurrection is central to Christianity and because we have four sets of narratives about it. Furthermore, these narratives are history-like in their narrative form and they do not seem to agree very well with one another. And to complicate matters, they are about events that have no parallels in our experience: appearances of someone alive who had died and was buried. So work began to be done on questions such as, did anyone know where Jesus' tomb was? Were there angels there on Easter morning? One or two, inside or outside, standing or sitting? (Sounds a little like an eye exam, doesn't it? -- which in a certain sense it was!). And what, if anything, did the angels say? Did Jesus really appear? Were the so-called witnesses hallucinating? Was their experience purely psychological? Did anyone really touch Jesus physically? Was the multiplication of appearances a case of psychological contagion? Were the narratives perhaps developed by a process of actualizing Old Testament prophecies and applying them to Jesus?[9] And on and on.

Why were these questions, and many more like them, which have spawned literally thousands of studies of the Resurrection over the last century, so engrossing, intriguing, even urgent? Quite simply, because the presuppositions characteristic of historical critical methods of studying ancient texts convinced biblical scholars that unless we could establish the objective facts about the Easter event, we had no solid historical, that is, objective basis for faith in the Resurrection. We might have other bases, for example, Church authority, tradition, or blind faith. But, for the modern scientifically oriented person, if Jesus rose from the dead, as the texts claim, then the objective facts, or the lack thereof, had to be established so that, on that basis, we could decide, theologically, what it all meant, what we are really justified in believing and on what grounds and what our options are if some things turn out not to be "true" in this factual sense.[10]

Even if we are sure a car crash happened, there is a huge difference, with all kinds of consequences, if the car crash was due to someone deliberately running the red light or to the fact that the brakes failed as the driver was trying to stop. Likewise, even if we are convinced for other reasons to believe in the Resurrection, it remains crucial to know if Jesus' tomb was empty, if anyone whose testimony was not biased actually checked it out or if this was just a rumor in support of a belief derived from other sources. And if the tomb was empty is this explained by his disciples' stealing the body during the night and spreading a story of resurrection, or by the fact that he was never buried in a secure tomb in the first place and the abandoned body was destroyed by predatory animals between Good Friday evening and Easter morning, or by the fact that Jesus actually rose from the dead? Or does it matter at all whether the tomb was empty, if we do not equate resurrection with resuscitation? And if the most incredible hypothesis is true, namely, that the tomb was empty because Jesus is risen, who saw it and how do we know their version is reliable? and so on… From here we can go on to ask if we are talking about a pure faith conviction, with no actual relation to human history; about the immortality of the soul presented in myth-like narratives about bodily resurrection; about the mythological origins of a world religion called Christianity; or about the kind of world-shattering reality the Church celebrates on Easter?

After extensive research on every conceivable aspect of the historical data about the Resurrection, we are not much further ahead today in regard to the objective historical facts than the disciples were on Easter Sunday when, in various ways, the first witnesses exclaimed, "He is risen," and "We have seen the Lord." In other words, the historical critical assumptions about what constitutes an "event" or a "happening," and which equate verifiable objective "facts" with "the truth," pretty much rule out the possibility of our ever establishing with scientifically convincing data most of what many have considered absolutely necessary if our faith in the Resurrection is to have a solid historical basis. In other words, almost none of the objective historical facts about the central reality in question are indisputably ascertainable.

Now, I have long worked with a personal, not very technical but quite fruitful, principle of theological research that goes something like this: "If diligent and persistent efforts by highly competent scholars to answer a critical theological question do not produce some progress toward a credible answer, you are probably asking the wrong question or asking the right question wrongly. Best to hit "reset" on your research keyboard." My way of hitting "reset" in regard to this question of what happened at Easter is to pursue another approach to the Resurrection Narratives, namely a phenomenologically-based literary, rather than historical critical one, because I am becoming convinced that it has a better chance of providing what we are looking for, namely, a well-founded, credible, spiritually motivating approach to the central mystery of our faith that could be "imaginatively plausible" to post-Enlightenment moderns.

# *An Alternate Approach: Phenomenological/ Literary Approach*

In order to launch this alternate approach I invite you to join me in an imaginative experience. I want you to experience the effect on your imagination of looking at a set of questions. We are not interested, at this point, in their answers any more than we have been interested in whether the traffic event was an accident or a crime. We are interested in the structure of the knowledge. Here are the questions:

What do we mean by 9/11? Why do we call it 9/11 instead of giving it a name like "The Gettysburg Address" or "The Academy Awards"? What really happened on 9/11? How do we know? Is 9/11 over?

Now, let me suggest some responses. Skipping, for a moment, the first question, what do we mean by 9/11? I would suggest that we call it 9/11 partly because we do not know what it means or what is most significant about it or even, about some aspects of what happened? We can probably agree that it is the day that two jet planes were deliberately flown into the World Trade Center in New York City. But that hardly accounts for the national trauma that is still reverberating through the country more than ten years later. After all, we've had plane crashes before and since. The terrorist, Timothy McVeigh, blew up a government building in Oklahoma City killing and injuring almost a 1,000 people just ten years before 9/11; fewer than 3,000 people died in the attack on 9/11;[11] in comparison, more than 16,000 people were murdered in the U.S. that same year. In other words, it is not a plane crash, terrorism, the number of violent deaths alone, or even all of them together that accounts for the traumatic effect of 9/11.

Furthermore, there are conflicting stories about what really went on inside the building that morning. Many of the eyewitness or participant stories conflict, or are impossible to jibe with each other, and at least 2500 stories were lost forever because they died with the victims who did not escape. We do not know what to call this phenomenon, 9/11, because we do not know, factually, exactly what happened; exactly what is and is not part of the event itself or simply collateral damage or unrelated side events that somehow got caught up in the drama, and so we do not know finally what it really means. Thus, we point to it by recalling the date. 9/11 designates, even for people too young to remember the day, "whatever it is that happened on that fateful date." 9/11 is a different kind of event from an automobile crash at Elm and Main, and not simply in physical magnitude.

Going a bit beyond the objective facts we can ascertain at that site, we get into what produced whatever happened which, in a sense, is more important if we want to understand the event. The pilots of the two planes were Islamic-connected terrorists—or at least that's what we called them. They, and the people they worked for, saw them as religious warriors, servants of Allah in the cause of justice and liberation of Islam from an anti-Muslim imperialist power that was already at war, economically, politically, and culturally, with Islam, namely, the United States. The mainstream U.S. story says they were operatives of a terrorist group called Al Qaeda and that they blew up the buildings from the outside from motives of extremist religious hatred and/or jealousy of America's superior culture, freedom, and economic strength. Conspiracy theorists, on the other hand, have long suspected that 9/11 was a "Pearl Harbor" operation, allowed or facilitated from within by the U.S. government, so that the American people could be deceived into going to war with Iraq, which had nothing to do with the attacks on the WTC, for government motives of acquisition of oil. In other words, causation in this case is not as simple as whether someone ran a red light or the brakes failed.

But things get even more complicated when we look not at what happened, or even at what produced the event, but at what the event produced. Almost overnight the freest nation in the world took on many of the aspects of a national security state, including the indefinite suspension of many cherished personal, civil, and political rights. The airline industry was set back decades. Behaviors long held by Americans to be utterly morally repugnant and violations of international law such as torture, were adopted by our government as necessary anti-terrorist methods. We became involved in the two longest wars in our history, neither of which has been "won" in any clear sense of that word. Thousands of U.S. service personnel are dead and tens of thousands maimed in mind and body. Hundreds of thousands of Iraqis and Afghans, mostly innocent women and children, have died at our hands. Many Americans have developed a deep-seated suspicion of Muslims that no amount of official condemnation of such bigotry can eradicate. And we cannot even begin to count the economic costs of 9/11. But there were also amazing stories of bravery, personal self-sacrifice, generosity, devotion. There was an upsurge in active patriotism among many who had taken American freedom for granted. And all of this does not begin to get the whole happening "out there" for objective consideration.

But in any case, it cannot be denied that the country is no longer, and many believe will never be again, what it was minutes before those jets hit the towers. Whatever 9/11 means, it is not over.

Let us go back, now, to our original historical critical questions: What do we mean by 9/11? Why do we call it 9/11, instead of giving it a name? What really happened? How do we know? Is 9/11 over? We might not be able to answer with certitude any of those questions and surely we do not agree on the answers we think we do have and no matter how many studies are written and reports published and films made and historical or literary versions proposed, we probably never will get the whole picture. We cannot stamp "Case closed" on this event like we will eventually be able to do with the car crash. But the one question we all would surely consider absurd is "Did anything really happen?"

Something momentous happened on September 11, 2001 and is still happening. A real event which infinitely overflows the boundaries of that one day in September, those two buildings, the comparatively small number of victims, the motivations of the attackers, the conflicting causation theories, the eye-witness stories that do not match, the evaluation of the ongoing official responses and the unofficial reactions, definitely happened. And, no matter what position one takes on any of these factual questions, 9/11 is full of meaning which we will be unpacking, sifting, arguing over, narrativizing, and ordering our lives in terms of, probably as long as there is a United States. It is an event, a reality, from which there is no going back. The overwhelming event has been generating and will continue to generate what the philosopher Hans Georg Gadamer called an "effective history", a progressive deepening of the event itself by what flows from it and back over it.[12]

Phenomenological philosophers talk of such events as "saturated phenomena",[13] events or experiences which burst their boundaries or our capacity to absorb them, which are so overwhelming that the mind reels and language stammers or tumbles over itself, and the excess of meaningfulness, positive, negative, or both, so overpowers our ability to absorb, sort, parse, respond that we use expressions like "mind-blowing" or "mind-boggling," or we speak of being "blown away." and do not really know what we mean by these terms except that the ordinary rational mind cannot handle the overload of significance that the event or happening mediates.

There are many such events in life, many of which are not public, national, or literally earth-shaking like an explosion or tsunami but which are genuinely overwhelming. Parents have written of their participation in the birth or death of their child. Naturalists have described events of vast, irremediable ecological devastation or of bare survival against superhuman physical odds. Some children have been victims of crimes so horrendous that memory of them is repressed beyond retrieval. And many people have tried to express life-changing religious conversion experiences. Language is so overpowered by the reality of these saturated phenomena that it is reduced to stammering. But those who read such accounts, whether in prose or poetry, also realize that the language itself, in its effort to approximate the event itself, both enriches and is enriched by the superabundance of reality impinging on consciousness.

With some other scholars currently working on the Resurrection, I would suggest that Easter was, quintessentially, a saturated event. It was so totally unexpected, overpowering, without analogue, dense, inexplicable that no one knew what to do or say, how or what to describe, what it meant or means. The first people confronted by the event were literally "blown away" by what they experienced.

Perhaps our earliest Gospel account, Mark 16:1-8, in its stark, enigmatic, original ending, is closest to the actual event. Mark says simply that the women who went to the tomb, expecting to find and anoint the corpse of Jesus, were suddenly confronted by a young man in white garments, sitting inside the previously sealed, but now gaping tomb, who announced to them, "You are looking for Jesus.... He has been raised; he is not here." The Gospel ends: the women "fled from the tomb, for terror and amazement had seized them; and they said nothing to anyone, for they were afraid" (Mk. 16:6-7). This does sound exactly like the first reaction to a saturated phenomenon. One simply has no categories with which to interpret it. It overwhelms perception, shutting down our ordinary capacities to deal with the matter. We cannot think of anything to say that will sound rational or that anyone will believe. We doubt our own senses. We may think we are losing our minds. We want to get far away so we can regroup, process what has happened, figure out what to say or how or if we should say anything at all.

In the other Gospels we get more circumstantial accounts, more description of the angelic messengers, references to the rolled back stone and an earthquake, slightly different words for "Whom do you seek?" or "He has been raised," references to fear and disbelief, running from the tomb, even seeing Jesus himself, reporting to the disciples who conclude the women are hysterical and who do not believe the report. But essentially, like the basically similar reports from different people who were at Ground Zero—of jets flying way too low, the deafening crash of the planes into the building, everything shuddering like an earthquake, blinding light and thick dust, screaming people fleeing in all directions, the basic data of Easter are fairly similar—of women coming to the tomb to anoint the body, the inexplicably open and empty tomb, the stunning unearthly messengers with the incredible news that the dead and buried Jesus is alive, the overwhelming effect on the women, their flight from the tomb, seeing Jesus, their report that the male disciples dismiss as simply incredible. Megaliths do not move of their own accord.

Angels do not appear in broad waking daylight delivering messages from beyond the grave. Dead people do not come back to life.

In both cases, there was a lot of inconsequential variation on the facts and the facts really did not explain anything anyway. But everyone involved knew that something momentous had happened and that there was general agreement on the phenomenological "what" that had happened: the Trade Center Towers were hit by airplanes, collapsed, killing hundreds or more and America was under attack; Jesus' body was gone, unearthly beings were in possession of the tomb, and he was declared risen from the dead and was even seen by some people.

At Easter, as in the aftermath of 9/11, the bare facts never changed much after the first reports. They were no more or less uniform in substance, no more or less explanatory. What did begin to develop in both cases were highly circumstantial vignettes of personal experiences: a first responder racing from the scene with a baby in his arms, a tender farewell message discovered on a cell phone, a man walking in a daze coated in white dust and still carrying a brief case as if there were something like "business as usual" to be resumed, a service dog leading his blind master out of what was left of the building. People wrote stories, essays, poems; others made films or painted pictures, catching, as it were through a crack in the enormity of the event, the immensity of what had happened. Makeshift shrines appeared and official ceremonies took place while eyewitnesses told their stories again and again, sometimes with fairly obvious self-contradictions and/or embellishments. Art, both popular and professional, which embodies the universal in the particular, and ritual which channels and shapes chaotic feeling too complex and overwhelming to be expressed in normal words and deeds and unites people beyond what they can understand or explain, were much more suited to capturing the stupendous reality than newspaper accounts or analytical articles or official police reports.

And that is the kind of thing we get in the Easter Narratives: vignettes of personal experiences: Peter and the Beloved disciple racing to the tomb, what they found inside, and Peter's befuddlement contrasted with the Disciple's quietly dawning, awe-struck belief; Mary Magdalene encountering Jesus in someone she took for the gardener and, on the spot, becoming the first apostle of the Risen Jesus; two disciples walking hopelessly home to Emmaus and meeting a mysterious Stranger who suddenly made himself known as they sat at table and then, just as suddenly, was gone; Jesus simply in the midst of the community locked away in fear; Thomas getting caught in his stubborn challenge to One he thought he would never see again; shared meals and conversations that were real but mysterious with Someone who did not exactly leave but who was suddenly no longer visible and then, elsewhere, was present again.

In other words, if the Easter experience was a prolonged saturated phenomenon, rather than a circumscribed single event like a car crash, accounts of it would have the kinds of characteristics in which saturated events come to expression. We would expect them to be not uniformly fact laden and minimalistic but overflowing, poetic, redundant, reflective of the mind-blowing intensity and richness of the experience itself. It may be only Mark's original ending that reflects rather directly the tomb event itself like the footage of the actual impact of the planes that was played over and over and really told the viewer nothing except that something mind-boggling had happened. The other Resurrection Narratives and even the longer appendix to Mark, were surely composed over a period of time and probably reflect not only the immediate experience of the 50 days between Easter and the Pentecost, but the way the stories were told and used in the interim between Easter and the writing of the Gospels. They are later, fuller, more variegated, less easily reduced to a single narrative, than the bare proclamations of the Resurrection we find in Paul and in Acts.

So, let us move from thinking about what the saturated event itself must have been like to the texts in which those events are narrated and the major feature of the Risen Jesus which these texts communicate because that is what later believers, like ourselves, have to work with.

# IV

# THE RESURRECTION IN TEXT AND IN CHRISTIAN EXPERIENCE

Most believers who raise questions about the Resurrection are not actually questioning the fact of the Resurrection itself that they take on faith. They are really asking how the testimony of the witnesses, as it came to be expressed in the texts in which the Easter events are recounted, is related to the event in question, that is, to the Resurrection experience of the earliest communities. Do these stories, which we have at the end of each of the Gospels, really tell us anything reliable, that is, objectively factual, about the Resurrection, about what happened, about the Risen Jesus himself, and so on? Do the stories, by their lack of agreement, diversity of perspectives, variety of facts, and so on, not cause more problems than they solve? Would we not be better off with a single straightforward narrative or even a simple proclamation, "He is risen," leaving us to imagine for ourselves whatever that might mean? I would suggest that the answer to that is no, for two reasons. First, the accounts themselves, even in or because of their diversity, are actually a warrant of credibility about the witnesses and their witness. Second, and even more importantly, the Resurrection Narratives are the primary resource for our faith not in the fact of the Resurrection, that it happened, but in the bodiliness of the Resurrection which is of supreme significance for our faith.

## *The Credibility of the Witnesses and the Texts*

Without stopping to discuss all the evidence I can report that there is a fairly wide scholarly consensus about what the textual material affirms on the following two points: the tomb and the appearances. And that consensus is the more reassuring precisely because the diversity in the narratives themselves highlights their consensus.

1. The tomb was empty on Easter morning. This does not say what that meant or how it happened but if the body of Jesus had been available the authorities, both political and religious, who had a high stake in nipping the Christian movement in the bud, could easily have done so by producing Jesus' corpse, or at least his remains. We have no record that the authorities ever credibly disputed the disciples' claim that the tomb was empty. And, in any case, although the empty tomb has other important meanings, the Church, even at the very beginning, never based faith in the Resurrection on the empty tomb.

2. In regard to the appearances there are several interesting facts about the witness to the Resurrection, easily derived from the narratives themselves regardless of what the narratives affirm about the Resurrection, which suggest that the witness itself is credible, i.e., trustworthy.

a. None of those to whom Jesus appeared are presented as expecting, hoping for, or seeking an appearance any more than the people going to work on 9/11 expected an attack on the World Trade Center. In each appearance case the recipient was in deep sorrow and despair over Jesus' obviously irreversible fate, his death. All were totally surprised,[14] even in some cases terrified, by his appearance. So we are not talking about expectation or wish fulfillment.

b. Although all the appearances were to Jesus' disciples who knew him well, not to strangers, none of the recipients recognized Jesus until Jesus somehow identified himself. So the witnesses were not inventing the appearances nor were they hallucinating.

c. None of the appearances duplicates any other. Although there are similar details that show up in one account or another, such as the wounds in Jesus' hands, each appearance is unique in time, place, circumstances, content, etc. So these were not "copy-cat" accounts.

d. All of the appearances happened in "real time" while the recipient was wide-awake and in ordinary circumstances. None are presented as visions, dreams, ecstasies, out-of-body experiences, bereavement encounters, or the like.

e. The appearances started on Easter morning and ceased completely at the end of a particular, relatively short, clearly delineated period of time, referred to as the "40 days" concluded by the Ascension, except that to Paul which both he and the others recognized as an exception. So the appearance stories are not dramatic ways of talking about ordinary Christian experiences of later times or "repeats" by those who had heard other reports. They are presented as accounts of absolutely sui generis events, neither produced by nor reproducible by the disciples and therefore in no way under their control.

In short, the appearances are presented as somehow "objective" in that they happened to, rather than being produced by, the recipients. Contrary to their expectations, Someone appeared to the witnesses, made himself known as Jesus, was recognized, interacted with the recipient, and disappeared without "exiting the scene" in any normal sense of the word. And each such experience was unique in form and content. These features of the appearances should lay to rest some of the questions which might sidetrack our use of this phenomenological approach. In other words, something happened and real people experienced it and there is enough consistency about what that experience was to justify questions about what it meant.

## Bodiliness of the Risen Jesus

Once we begin to realize that there is no possibility of, nor point in, trying to match up the Resurrection accounts point for point in order to establish the objective "facts" as if the Resurrection were a car accident, we can begin to read these narratives on their own merits as overflowing witness to an overwhelming saturated phenomenon in which the first disciples participated intensely during a limited privileged period called the "forty days." This period of the revelation of the Paschal Mystery came to a close with the withdrawal of Jesus' sensible presence from them in the Ascension and his definitive interior return to them in the Spirit on Pentecost. The episodes recorded are not quasi-police reports. They are mini-dramas, short stories, poetic discourses, or verbal paintings reflective of the reality of what happened to the participants during the relatively short period from Easter morning to the outpouring of the Spirit at Pentecost which empowered them to make available to the "whole world" the life, death, and Resurrection of Jesus through their life in community, their preaching, their writing, their ritual.

During this foundational period which we might call the Pascal Event, this saturated event of Jesus' bodily return to his disciples, his departure from their sight, his taking up his indwelling presence within and among them, Jesus was vividly present to them, teaching them; opening their eyes to really "see", that is to deeply understand, what they had seen physically in his public life, passion and death; opening their ears to "hear" what the Scriptures say in relation to what Jesus had said to them before and after his execution; supporting them in their fears; feeding them; correcting them; forgiving them; empowering them; sending them. He was there day after day. He came to them in Jerusalem and in Galilee, in closed rooms and on the road and at the seashore, to individuals and to groups, in familiar ways and new ways (see Acts 1:3-4). He flooded them with his nearness, his presence, his intimacy. They could not mistake who it was. John says, "Now none of the disciples dared to ask him, "Who are you?" because they knew it was the Lord." (Jn. 21:12). He came to them and came again, but he never left. They saw and heard and touched and knew that it was Jesus himself, alive, returned to them, but not in their power because he was no longer subject to the constraints of time and space and the ordinary laws of causality. They needed to learn by experience what his new presence felt like, how to recognize it, what it meant for them.

And once the Spirit, whom Jesus had promised would be for them what he had been during his public life, had come upon them they immediately began, first by preaching and proclamation, and eventually by the writing of what we now call the New Testament, to share their experience and to invite others to enter into it. Their witness was contagious. Immediately, according to Acts, thousands heard, mysteriously understanding the meaning even when the speaker's language was not their own, and they asked, "What should we do? How can we participate in this new life that is pouring out of you the way exuberance pours out of someone drunk on new wine?" (cf.Acts 2:4-18).

The disciples not only preached but began to develop rituals by which others could become participants. They invited their hearers to take part in a mystical plunging into the death of Jesus from which they would rise with eyes "enlightened" to perceive God's work in Jesus, and ears "opened" to understand Jesus' word, and tongues "loosed" for praise and proclamation. The disciples invited these newly baptized to share table fellowship with them, to do with them what Jesus had commanded: to wash one another's feet (Jn. 13:1-15), to share bread and wine in remembrance of him (see Lk. 22.:19-20), and to form inclusive community. The New Testament Resurrection Narratives and the Easter sacraments of Baptism and Eucharist are the witness in word and ritual to the overwhelming Paschal Mystery of Jesus' Resurrection and the outpouring of the Spirit.

A striking feature of this participation in the saturated event of the Paschal Mystery was its totally egalitarian inclusivity. The Easter appearances were to women and men, members of the Twelve and of the Seventy-two and crowds of hundreds; to ordinary disciples like the two, probably an ordinary married couple, on their way home to Emmaus, and those, members of the Twelve and others without names (see Jn. 21:2), who were with Simon in the boat on the Sea of Tiberias. The Spirit was poured out equally, in identical individual tongues of fire, without distinction or rank, on the whole gathered community of 120, including the Mother of Jesus and the Twelve, who were together in prayer between the Ascension and Pentecost. The Paschal Event was an ecclesial foundation, the coming to life of the Body of Christ born from the open side of the Crucified Jesus, not the establishment of an institution or the creation of hierarchically mediated mechanisms of salvation. All that came later. And, as the disciples began to welcome others into this experience, they realized that, in a way that transcended the First Covenant, it was intended for all: women as well as men, Jews of the Diaspora as well as of Palestine, proselytes as well as Israelites, Gentiles as well as Jews, slaves as well as free, young as well as old, poor as well as rich.

Underlying, and making possible, the absolute conviction of the disciples about the reality of the Risen Jesus and his presence among and in them, and central to the preaching and rituals by which they facilitated the conversion of others, was the most striking feature of the narratives themselves which grounded the continuity between the earthly life of Jesus among his pre-Easter disciples and his new life within his Paschal community. Herein lies the ultimate significance of the Easter experience. All the Easter Narratives are stories about Jesus himself present bodily. In this respect, the Resurrection Narratives are not just artistic or imaginative productions reflecting a saturated phenomenon. They have a very particular content that is central to the revelation of the Resurrection.

The first witnesses, in their Easter experiences, knew that they had encountered the Jesus they knew prior to his death not simply as a vivid memory, a figment of the imagination, an hallucination, a spirit or ghost or immortal soul, or even as a kind of "apparition" like the spectre of Samuel conjured up for Saul by the Witch of Endor (I Sam. 28:3–25). Jesus himself, in the appearance to the disciples in Luke 24:37-43, forecloses that sort of interpretation of their experience by saying "Look at my hands and my feet; see that it is I myself. Touch me and see; for a ghost [which is what they thought they were seeing] does not have flesh and bones as you see that I have." And as they remained uncertain he asked, "'Have you anything here to eat?' They gave him a piece of broiled fish, and he took it and ate in their presence." In other words, Christian faith does not merely affirm that Jesus is alive with God, nor simply that in some sense he is still with us. It claims that Jesus is bodily risen, or that the Risen Jesus is bodily. He can be seen, heard, touched. We believe in the resurrection of the body.

Some people think it would be much easier to deal with and present the challenge of Christian faith if we could finesse that insistence on the body, proclaim that Jesus is alive, immortal, with God, influencing us, and so on but agree that after his death his body went the way of all flesh, namely, that it returned to the earth and was reabsorbed into the cosmic process as are all our bodies after we die. Why cling to this extraordinary notion of bodily resurrection which poses even logistical problems such as where can the bodies of the billions of people who have died be, physically, now or for all eternity? And, how do we solve such problems as the result of organ transplants when the heart in question has belonged to two different people, and so on? In one sense, we would like to dismiss these questions themselves as conundrums that just muddy the waters of faith with outlandish speculations on which no real light is shed by imagination or reason.

If Jesus himself and his first disciples, thought that the issue of his bodily resurrection was critical to Christian faith we need to take the issue seriously. Paul, our earliest written witness to the Resurrection, had to deal with it head on in relation to his Corinthian converts. They asked, when he preached to them on the Resurrection, "How are the dead raised? With what kind of body do they come?" (1 Cor. 15:35). Paul did not brush off their questions as naïve or unimportant. The first question that has to be answered is, does it really make any difference whether the resurrection of Jesus was bodily or not and, if so, what does bodily mean?

Yes, it makes a huge difference, for two reasons, both extremely simple and extremely important. First, our bodies are not just houses in which we dwell, or shells, or husks, or even, as Socrates taught, the prison of the soul. No, our body is ourself. We do not say, for example, "Do not hit my arm," or " My body feels sick," but "Do not hit me" or "I am sick." In more technical language, one's body, and all its extensions in our actions, our words, our creations, our ideas, even our projects and the communities in which we participate and so on are the symbolic way of being oneself in the world.

A symbol is not a sign, that is, something that stands for something other than itself the way an exit sign stands for a door. (If you move the exit sign the door does not cease to exist and the place you put the sign does not become a way out.) A real symbol is a way of being present of something that cannot otherwise be present. It is not a stand-in for something that is absent but the bodying-forth of a transcendent reality that is present. That is the very reason why, according to the Judaeo-Christian tradition, God could only reveal God-self to the people Israel through creation, history, persons, words, mighty acts. God, utterly transcendent, can only reveal Godself to humans by, as it were, speaking "human", that is, coming to us symbolically. The final, greatest, only complete and adequate self-revelation of God is the Word of God become incarnate in Jesus. Jesus, as bodily, that is, as human, is the great symbol of God, not as a representative of God but as Godself. If, in death, Jesus had ceased to be his bodily self he would not simply have laid aside a temporary "vestment" or container of some sort. He would have ceased to be a human being, that is, to be himself, Jesus, the One in whom our humanity participates in Trinitarian life and which makes that Trinitarian life present to us. In short, if Jesus had ceased to be a bodily human being, what we call the Incarnation, God's becoming one of us that we might become one with God, would have ceased. So the first reason why the bodiliness of the Resurrection is so important is that it is intrinsic to Jesus integral humanity. Only as bodily could Jesus rise as himself, and not as a trace or reminder of himself. Bodiliness is what keeps us continuous with ourselves no matter how much we change over time and even through death.

The second reason derives from the first. Bodiliness is the mysterious feature of our humanity by which we are always simultaneously both present and absent, both related to all creation and distinct from all else. My body marks me off from all other humans, makes me myself in the face of all other reality, establishes me in my individuality, locality, and causality. No one else is me and I am not anyone else. The symbol which effects and manifests that distinctiveness is my body. By leaving the scene, bodily, I can absent myself from others and conversely, by coming bodily into the situation, whether physically or electronically or intellectually or emotionally or by my work or my participation, or in some other way, I become present.

Because of our bodiliness we can enter into relationships potentially with all other beings. Through our body we can see and hear and touch and taste and smell what is other than ourself. We can be part of a community. We can influence others by words and gestures and actions. Our experience of the death of a loved one is precisely that presence is overwhelmed by absence in the moment when the body ceases to mediate the person, ceases to symbolically body-forth the person in this context. We no longer call the fleshly trace in the coffin a "body," but a "corpse" which is the symbolic presence of an absence, the way absence is made present or the person is experienced as absent. That is why a corpse is so mysterious, commands such reverence, even inspires fear. In death the body is trans-symbolized so that what had made the person present now makes the person absent.

Jesus' body is no less important, significant, symbolic for him than ours is for us. Jesus was present to his pre-Easter contemporaries as his bodily self-rendering God symbolically present. The Church has always claimed that Jesus' death was not a charade, a piece of theater. He really died. His bodiliness, which had made him symbolically, that is, really, present to his contemporaries became a corpse which made his absence symbolically, that is, really, present to those who buried him. Jesus was gone, as completely and truly as is any person when who dies, and his body, now become a corpse, was the symbolic expression of that transformation from life to death, from presence to absence.

Therefore, if Jesus, after his death, is truly to return to his own, to be really humanly present to and in and among them, to be able to speak to them, act in and on them, energize them, relate to them, he can only do this through his bodily Resurrection. But, and this is supremely important, Jesus does not just come "back to life." He does not re-animate his corpse. He is not resuscitated which would just have made it necessary for him to die again and Paul said emphatically, "Death no longer has dominion over him" (Rom. 6:9). Rather, as we struggle for words for this transformation we might say that the finite character (what Scripture tends to call "the flesh") of Jesus' earthly life which limited his divinity by mortality as all mortals are limited, was swallowed up in his very real death into the infinite life of God. This divine humanity, which is bodily because it is human, and which had always been his, took complete possession of his being even visibly. What was glimpsed for a moment on Tabor in the Transfiguration is now totally and definitively and absolutely revealed. It does not obliterate Jesus' humanity but it transfigures it, transsymbolizes it, or to use the traditional language, glorifies it. The Jesus who rose from the tomb was not the earthly, physical Jesus resuscitated but the incarnate Son of God glorified. We need to learn how to think of bodiliness not as equivalent to physicality but as the special way of being present of humans. All the humans we know are bodily as physical but physicality, as the Resurrection teaches us, is not of the essence of human bodiliness.

The Resurrection appearance narratives and Paul's experience of the Risen Jesus give us a kind of repertoire of language and images by which to think about, appreciate, grasp what glorification of the body, or Resurrected life means. Together they signify that the person, who lives as bodily glorified, although continuous with him or herself, is in a different relationship to presence and absence than is the mortal or fleshly human being.

When we line up all the unusual, beyond mortal or earthly, features in the Easter Narratives we have a whole collection of seemingly incompatible affirmations. Jesus can be simultaneously present to people in different, even widely separated, geographical places, for example, eating with the disciples in Emmaus and appearing to Simon in Jerusalem (see Lk. 24:30-34). He can be present to people who knew him well, like Mary Magdalene, and not be recognizable to them (Jn. 20:14-16) but he can become recognizable when he chooses to be even to people who never met him "in the flesh" like Paul (see Acts 9:4-5). He is not impeded by solid, physical barriers, as in his sudden presence among the disciples in the locked room in Jerusalem (see Jn.

20: 19). He can but does not have to eat as he demonstrated to the disciples together in Jerusalem in Luke (24:36-43) and to the disciples in Emmaus (see Lk. 24:30-31). He knows where people, like Thomas, are and what they are thinking and saying when he is apparently not present (see Jn. 20:24-28). With or without words he can open people's minds to the inner meaning of Scripture, which, though written before he was born, clearly refers to himself (Lk. 24:25-27, 32). And throughout Christian history He can make himself present to people visibly as he did to Teresa of Avila but also in other ways such as in the intimacy of a shared meal, or the insistent inspiration of a vocation, or making our work superabundantly fruitful when we had exhausted all our human capabilities.

In other words, a glorified body is not just a mortal body that glows in the dark. Glorification is a condition of bodiliness, which renders it not limited by space or time or the type of causality that governs physical reality in our space-time continuum, but which can act effectively in that context. The Risen Jesus lives in God, not in our physical condition of materiality, but in a glorified materiality which, on the one hand, enables him to participate in our mortal reality as he wills but also leaves him free of its limitations, all of which are in some way the cause, effect, or expression of mortality. Thus the early Church captured the meaning of the bodily Resurrection of Jesus by saying not only that he was alive, but that "Death no longer has dominion over him." And if death has no power over him that is because those things that lead to death have ceased to affect him. He cannot starve, be killed, grow old because change has become irrelevant. This is not something we can easily fathom or imagine. We are talking about genuine bodiliness in which the body as flesh, that is, as mortal, does not control the spirit but the spirit controls, uses, acts through and by means of materiality in whatever way is needed. This is why it is probably not very helpful to speak of Jesus' bodiliness as physical or fleshly, because physicality, precisely, denotes that aspect of bodiliness which is subject to change, decay, death. We would probably be speaking more clearly if we talked of Jesus' glorified body as material, that is, able to interact with all that we mean by matter in this world, but not as itself flesh or mortal. Glorification means no longer subject to death nor anything which leads to death, results from death, or expresses death. Glorification is not the eradication of the body; it is the end of subjection to death.

# Conclusion

Everything we have been discussing is marvelously concentrated in the Lukan story of the disciples on the way to Emmaus (Lk 24:13-35). A little community of Jesus' utterly discouraged and despairing disciples, Cleopas and quite probably his wife,[15] are trudging dejectedly home from the scene of Jesus' execution and as they talk about him, their minds clouded by grief and hopelessness, Someone is with them. As they include him in their conversation the tenor of their conversation subtly begins to change. From wallowing in sadness they begin to experience glimmers of understanding, hope, possibility, transformation, an inner Spirit burning away the negativity and despair and paralysis as the Scriptures enlighten the awful experiences of the past few days -- so much so that they press him to stay with them. They sit down to dinner, still trying to understand more deeply the Scriptures that seemed to open in new ways in his presence. And suddenly they realize that this Stranger is no stranger. As they break bread together they realize that this is Bread is not just bread and that their relationship is no ordinary Community.

Inflamed with his Spirit they rush back to Jerusalem to share with the rest of the Church what they now know from their own experience: Jesus is alive. And they hear from the others the echo of their own experience, that he has appeared also to Simon, and to others. And over the days, and down through the centuries, the stories keep coming in. I saw him. He spoke to me. He is with us. He is not dead. Death has no hold on him nor, because of him, on us. Jesus is alive! Alleluia!

# NOTES

\* The research for this lecture was supported in part by the Henry Luce Foundation through the Henry Luce III Fellows in Theology Program of the Association of Theological Schools.

1 I am borrowing this notion of "imaginative plausibility" from a reference in Gerald O'Collins, *Jesus Risen: An Historical, Fundamental and Systematic Examination of Christ's Resurrection* (New York/Mahwah: Paulist, 1987), p. 131 where he refers to John Henry Newman's "insistence that the reasonableness of faith entails its being credible for our imagination."

2 I am using the term "Easter" for the inauguration of the Paschal Mystery (which itself extends from Jesus' Crucifixion through his Resurrection, Ascension, and Pentecost) not to denote a day or date. Whatever we mean by "the Resurrection" began between Jesus' death on Calvary on Friday and the finding of the empty tomb by the women witnesses on the Sunday morning after the Sabbath. So, when I speak of "Easter" I am not intending to say that whatever I am discussing actually happened on Sunday. The meaning of "happened" is part of the burden of this essay.

3 The Englightenment, extending from the mid-seventeenth to the end of the eighteenth century, was an intellectual revolution in the west, which had ramifications in the political, social, economic, and ecclesiological spheres. The Enlightenment championed the reign of reason over the medieval reign of faith. This led eventually to the rationalism, scientism, and materialism that have raised problems for any kind of faith not based on the experimental, the observable, the demonstrable. Obviously, not all people or institutions embraced the extremes of the Enlightenment approach. And much in that approach constituted a genuine advance over the credulity that often posed as faith.. But the ethos of the Enlightenment influenced western thought

profoundly and set up criteria of proof, certitude, etc. which eroded at least the ease of basing knowledge on faith which was "normal" in the Middle Ages, and undermined the intellectual framework which made much of Catholic faith intellectually available to many Christians.

4  The basic English language biblical text I am using is the NRSV. However, at times I use my own translation and often cite eliptically to give the sense of a passage without citing it in full. The references in parentheses will guide the reader to the location for the full text.

5  The Greek text has both verbs in the present tense: "I go away and I come to you" or "I am going away and I am coming to you" rather than, as many translations suggest "I am going away and [then] I will come back to you."

6  For definition and explanation of "midrash," see Paul J. Actemeier, ed., et al. *The Harper Collins Bible Dictionary* (San Francisco, CA: Harper, c.1996. s.v.).

7  The Renaissance refers to the pan-European transitional movement, beginning in the 14th century in Italy and lasting into the 17th century, during which the Medieval world gave way to the Modern. It was marked by a humanistic revival of classical influence in general, and in the area of literature entailed a study of ancient texts which required the development of new methods of interpretation based on knowledge of the original languages, the study of ancient history in all its dimensions, attention to ancient cultures and so on.

8  The modern bibliography on the Resurrection (i.e., since 1950) is too vast to even indicate and much of it is in foreign languages. I give a fairly complete overview of the bibliographic sources in Sandra M. Schneiders, I.H.M., "The Resurrection (of the Body) in the Fourth Gospel: A Key to Johannine Spirituality" n.4, in *Life in Abundance: Studies of John's Gospel in tribute to Raymond E. Brown, S.S.*, edited by John R. Donahue, S.J. (Collegeville, MN: Liturgical Press, 2005), pp. 168-198. For recent English language bibliography see the "Select Bibliography" in Anthony J. Kelly, *The Resurrection Effect: Transforming Christian Life and Thought* (Maryknoll, NY: Orbis, 2008) and the copious notes in Brian D. Robinette, *Grammars of Resurrection* (New York: Crossroad, 2009).

9   For good examples of these types of studies see *The Resurrection: An Interdisciplinary Symposium on the Resurrection of Jesus*, edited by Stephen T. Davis, Daniel Kendall, and Gerald O'Collins (Oxford: Oxford University Press, 1997); *Resurrection: Theological and Scientific Assessments*, edited by Ted Peters, Robert John Russell, and Michael Welker (Grand Rapids, MI: Eeredmans, 2002); *The Resurrection of Jesus Christ*, edited by Paul Avis (London: Darton, Longman and Todd, 1993). Very recent studies which are deeply involved in the more polemical issues include *The Resurrection of Jesus : John Dominic Crossan and N.T. Wright in Dialogue*, edited by Robert B. Stewart (Minneapolis, MN: Fortress Press, 2006) as well as work of the Jesus Seminar on the historical Jesus.

10  A classic example of a study written to deal specifically with this set of questions is Gerd Lüdemann in collaboration with Alf Özen, *What Really Happened to Jesus: A Historical Approach to the Resurrection*, trans. by John Bowden (Louisville, KY: Westminster John Knox, 1995).

11  The actual current estimate is 2,753 killed of whom 1634, or 59%, have been identified.

12  I have explained Gadamer's notion of "effective historical consciousness" at some length in Sandra M. Schneiders, *The Revelatory Text: Interpreting the New Testament as Sacred Scripture*, revised and enlarged (Collegeville, MN: Liturgical, 1999), esp. in chapters 3 and 6.

13  For an excellent introduction to the notion of "saturated event" in relation to the Resurrection, see Anthony Kelly, *The Resurrection Effect*, Chapter 2, "A Phenominological Approach to the Resurrection." For an introduction to the work of Jean-Luc Marion who developed this category, see Brian Robinette, "A Gift to Theology? Jean-Luc Marion's 'Saturated Phenomenon' in Christological Perspective," *Heythrop Journal* 48 (2007): 86-108.

14  The most recent analysis of the Resurrection appearances including analyses of the accounts individually and collectively is Gerald O'Collins, *Believing in the Resurrection: The Meaning and Promise of the Risen Jesus* (New York/Mahwah,

NJ: Paulist, 2012), chapter 3, "The Appearances of the Risen Jesus" and the Appendix, "Easter Appearances and Bereavement Experiences."

15 In John 19:25 we are told that Mary, the wife of Clopas, was at the foot of the Cross with the Mother of Jesus and Mary Magdalene. If Mary of Clopas was part of the extremely intimate circle of women who accompanied the Mother of Jesus to the Cross, she was no doubt a prominent member of the earliest Christian community, a follower, with her husband, of the pre-Easter Jesus. Also, since the couple invited Jesus to stay overnight with them, it seems likely that they were a married couple since adult men would probably not have been single and would have been most unlikely to have been sharing a home. The most reasonable hypothesis is that Clopas (or Cleopas) was part of a married couple who were disciples of Jesus.

**Front and backcover Images**: Melisende Psalter

Though Queen Melisende's Psalter is probably not the earliest manuscript preserved from the Crusader Kingdom, it represents Crusading illumination of the early period at its best. From details within the psalter we know its place of origin to be the Church of the Holy Sepulchre in Jerusalem, and we can also date it fairly accurately between 1131 and 1143.

The image is reproduced with the permission of the British Library.

## Sandra M. Schneiders, IHM

Sister Sandra M. Schneiders has been a member of the Sisters, Servants of the Immaculate Heart of Mary since 1956. She received an M.A. In Philosophy from the University of Detroit in 1967; an S.T.L. in Patristics from Institut Catholique, Paris in 1971; and an S.T.D. In scripture and spirituality from Gregorian University, Rome in 1975.

She is currently professor of New Testament and spirituality at the Jesuit School of Theology and the Graduate Theological Union in Berkeley, California. She has written numerous articles and several books, including: *Selling All: Commitment, Consecrated Celibacy, and Community in Catholic Religious Life* (2001); *Finding the Treasure: Locating Catholic Religious Life in a New Ecclesial and Cultural Context* (2000); *With Oil in Their Lamps: Faith, Feminism, and the Future* (2000); *Written That You May Believe: Encountering Jesus in the Fourth Gospel* (2003); *and The Revelatory Text: Interpreting the New Testament as Sacred Scripture* (1999).

She is the recipient of three honorary degrees and the Christian Culture Gold Medal of Assumption University in Canada. In 2006, she won the John Courtney Murray Award, the highest honor bestowed by the Catholic Theological Society of America. She is past president of the Society for the Study of Christian Spirituality. From 2011-2013 she was a Luce Fellow. Her professional interests include New Testament literature, particularly Johannine literature and biblical hermeneutics, and Christian spirituality, particularly biblical spirituality, feminism, religious life and the theory of the field of spirituality.

At the 2012 Leadership Conference of Women Religious assembly, she was presented with its highest honor, the LCWR Outstanding Leadership Award.

She has lectured throughout the United States, Canada, Taiwan, and New Zealand.

## Mary Milligan RSHM

Sister Mary Milligan was born on January 23, 1935 in Los Angeles, California. She entered the RSHM Novitiate in New York and was later sent to the International Novitiate in Béziers, France. She earned a B.A. in French at Marymount College in Tarrytown, N.Y. in 1956; an M.A. in sacred scripture at St. Mary's College in Indiana in 1966; a Ph.D. in English at the L'Université de Paris in 1959; in 1975, she was the first woman to receive her Doctorate at the prestigious Pontifical Gregorian University in Rome. Her dissertation on the Spirit-Charism of Father Jean Gailhac provided a solid foundation for future research and study of RSHM history and spirituality. In 1988 she was awarded an honorary doctorate from Marymount University in Arlington Virginia. She published numerous articles on subjects such as scripture, women in religion, spirituality, and the relationship between feminism and religion. She spoke and wrote in several languages and she traveled extensively as part of her teaching, leadership, and scholarship; she was a leader in the Church, and represented the needs of women both locally and globally.

Mary was elected Councilor during the second mandate of Sister Margarida Maria Gonçalves. In 1975, and at the request of Sister Maria de Lourdes Machado, Mary coordinated process of revising the Constitutions of the Institute. A Special Commission and Mary gave the Constitutions their final form. The document was accepted by the Vatican in its first draft. In 1980 the General Chapter elected Mary as the 10th General Superior of the Institute of the Religious Sacred Heart of Mary.

Mary was a participant in the International Synod on the Laity in Rome (1987) and she was one of the prime movers of the Synod process for the Diocese of Los Angeles (1987-9), for which she co-wrote the final draft, a document which would outline the direction of the Diocese in the years to come. In 1986 Mary moved to Loyola Marymount University. She assumed many roles at LMU, including Professor of Theology; Provost (1986–1989); and Dean of the College of Liberal Arts (1992-1997). She died on April 2, 2011 at the age of 76.